K.E.Y.S

K.E.Y.S

(KEEP EDUCATING YOURSELF INTO SUCCESS PASSION AND PURPOSE)

Unlock Your Door

JAMIE CLARK

Palmetto Publishing Group
Charleston, SC

K.E.Y.S (Keep Educating Yourself into Success Passion and Purpose) Unlock Your Door

First Edition

Printed in the United States

ISBN-13: 978-1-64111-912-2
ISBN-10: 1-64111-912-8

INTRODUCTION

Are you ready for this book? I want to take you all on a journey. I want to define success after thirty and break it down. I plan to take you all on my journey yet focus on your own—with my help.

With that being said, I just turned thirty-one and have been on a whirlwind ride to success. As I begin to process where I am in life and where I would like to be, I plan to make some changes and have answers in thirty days.

There are words that we all know have a direct correlation with success, so throughout this book I would love to explore these words and mantras; we will break each down throughout this process.

Allow me to tell you all about who I am. I am a thirty-one-year-old mother of one and a fiancée. I currently manage in the hospitality industry, where I've worked since I was eighteen years old. In all, that's about thirteen years of service. At times I love it. I get to meet new people and consistently challenge myself daily. Recently, I was off work for four weeks due to an injury at work. This led me to idle time, social media laughs, and overall, my thoughts.

I realized I was under pressure, experiencing stress, anxiety, and some depression at times—80 percent of which was work related. I would scroll through social media, watching the lives of friends, celebrities, and people I didn't know go by. This allowed me to think about where my life was headed. Everyone seemed to be living life—don't get me wrong; I know everyone is happy on social media: right, that's the purpose of social media. This is where it all begins. I looked at comedians, those of my friends who were event planners, nurses, doctors, the ones raving about going back to school, etc.

This particular day I thought of all the things I said I wanted to do, and I decided to list them. To go with the list, I made a vision board too (I believe you should write things down in their entirety so that they will manifest fully).

I wanted—and actually started—a dope T-shirt line. I wanted—or *want*; let's say that instead. I *want* to be a general manager in the hotel industry. I want to own my own hotel. I want to write a book. I want to talk to exciting people and pick their brains.

Through this process, I learned I love how the mind works and how we all think differently. Here we are. I just had an interview earlier in the week. I'm hoping and praying I get this new job, but also starting these thirty days of affirmation and defining success. I have also started internalizing my thoughts and fears, and overall evaluating my journey, which I believe has pointed me in the right direction of success—because we all just want to be successful, right?

Day 1

FOCUS

The first word I want to dive into on my journey is focus. I tend to tell myself that if I can focus on one thing, I can accomplish many. In order to be successful, you have to be able to perfect one thing before moving on to the next. I would like to identify the things that throw me off my focus. Hmm? Good question: What is it that really throws me off my focus?

For me, life in general throws off my focus. I am sure you have this issue as well, but that is why it is called life. As I stated earlier, I am a fiancée as well as a mother. I have to create a balance between being a good mother and a soon-to-be wife. I have to find ways to communicate with my fiancé that are not just about our daughter and keep the relationship between us exciting and youthful. At times I lose focus within the relationship because I'm focusing on what our child is in need of at that moment. My focus can be off when I am consumed with the negative attributes of work. Upon me identifying some of the things that I lack focus on, I want you to also think deeper about your challenges as I begin to create tools to help me regain my focus.

What are some good tools that help me focus more? I'm glad you asked! It would be time management. Lists seem to work very well for me. I am one of those messy-organized people. Meaning I have no sense of numerical or alphabetical organizational skills, but I can tell you exactly where something is or where it should be. Pure chaos.

Allow us to take the time to get focused on the process ahead. For the next five days I am going to focus on all of my ventures, picking one day to dedicate to each individually.

Today I met with my group for our YouTube channel (Sh*ddd Let's Talk). It was very refreshing, I was focused, and I felt like I stuck to something and got it done. In order to make progress, take things one day at a time and allow things to unfold into the next step. Do not rush; everything takes times to create.

At times I make excuses as to why I don't get certain things done. I have to make the necessary changes and just do them, but that's what I'm focusing on within this journey: to do better to figure out what I am going to change and grasp a better understanding of it internally to make this a great journey. I will also write in my journal to set my goals for the New Year. Focus on the journey. Focus on what is important.

I want you to figure out what throws your focus off and determine how you will eliminate your focus-throwers one by one, day by day. One thing I know I have to do is focus, shut out the outside world, zoom in on me. It is OK to only think about me, my goals, and my ambition. I want you who are reading this book to write down what throws off your focus.

This is my list:

1. Working with difficult people
2. My two year old (she's unpredictable)
3. Life itself
4. Daily chores
5. Being tired
6. Social media
7. Senseless conversations

What's your list?

1. ____________________

2. ____________________

3. ____________________

4. ____________________

5. ____________________

6. ____________________

7. ____________________

How will I eliminate the seven things on this list or monitor them so that I can become more focused? Difficult people I can choose to walk away from, and I do not have to indulge in situations with difficult people. In my job I do have to talk to difficult people daily, but I do not have to allow it to consume my energy. I have learned that ten minutes of meditation allows me to eliminate negative energy. It is up to you to decide what is worth your energy.

My two year old is going to be my biggest challenge, but I have been working on a consistent schedule for her so that she is on a routine. I believe if I create a routine for her my ability to focus will become a lot better. It is all a working progress.

Life in general is an off-balancing experience, but choosing what you will allow in your vicinity is a start. Life is the one thing that will go haywire whenever, however—we cannot just control all of the ins and outs of life; it is impossible. We can control how we find balance and how we maintain our household daily. This goes back to me knowing I do well with lists and utilizing lists to my full advantage. I need weekly lists since they help me focus my attention and stay on track. No matter how much life gets out of hand, that list will keep me focused.

Time management, all in all, will be a major part of my journey to help me FOCUS! In order to get to the next level of whatever the achievement is, focusing on the task and the journey ahead will allow me, you, and everyone else who wants it badly enough, to be as successful as they would like to become.

Day 2

DISCIPLINE

It is day two and the word of this day is discipline. Day one we discussed being focused. With being focused there comes a sense of discipline. According to the dictionary, discipline means the practice of training people to obey rules and/or a code of behavior; using punishment to correct disobedience. Discipline, to me, is creating a routine I can stick to.

Success calls for making the decision to do or not to do. In my decision-making process I tend to lack discipline because I now know I lack focus. When I gain the focus I then can train my thoughts or my processes to become disciplined.

Now I'm questioning myself as I write this down to you. I mentioned trying to create a solid routine for myself. I don't mean the day-to-day stuff like going to work, etc. I mean time management. When I was younger, my father would make my brother and I iron all of our school clothes on Sunday night for the week. Discipline: the will to stay focused on the task and continually do.

I am thirty-one years old, and most weekends I try to visit my father after church on Sundays because this has become routine for me. It is also a part of me being disciplined in my routine. My nephew lives with my dad, and sure enough, on Sundays my dad irons his clothes and makes my nephew do the same. I have witnessed this for twenty-three years; that is true discipline. What my dad did and is doing is creating time management skills; he created routine, focus, and discipline.

A light bulb just went off as I am writing. That's my start: this Sunday I will get my daughter's clothing for school ready for the week. The journey is about the start. If I don't start, I will never finish anything.

As I reclaim my focus and my discipline, it takes me starting and finding the ways to my success. By preparing us for the week I free up my time. In order to focus on my crafts and ventures, I need the time. The thirty minutes I waste looking for our clothes in the morning is an hour wasted, due to having to look for the clothes and then iron them (wasting time). The goal is to not waste time, but only manage to it a lot better than I have done.

When we create habits that will allow us to not waste so much idle time, we start to witness things being taken care of. We all want to see tasks on our plate being completed. By becoming disciplined in our work, we create drive and will to continue pressing forward, even when everything seems mundane.

I will list my favorite quotes that will allow your brain to really dive into what it means to be disciplined, and hopefully it starts the juices flowing into the stream of success.

1. "Your level of success is determined by your level of discipline and perseverance." —unknown

2. "No discipline seems pleasant at the time, but painful. Later on, however, it produces a harvest of righteousness and peace for those who have been trained by it." —Hebrews 12:11

3. "Motivation will die; let discipline take its place." —unknown

4. "One of the most important keys to success is having the discipline to do what you know you should do, even when you don't feel like doing it." —unknown

5. "Small disciplines repeated with consistency every day lead to great achievements gained slowly over time." —John Maxwell

Day 3

SACRIFICES

Sacrifices. So far, we have openly discussed focus and the things I want to change that will eventually help my growth. I'm learning that I will have to sacrifice my time, my sleep, and my wants. Definitely my wants.

For instance, I have an app on my phone. It basically looked at my last four months in the year 2019 and gave me a brief synopsis of my spending habits from my main account. As I came up with obtainable goals for 2020, one of which was to save money. According to this app, I'm off to the wrong start. It stated that in three days of the New Year I already spent 130 percent more than I did in the month of December—crazy, right! This is the same app that told me I spent 30K in four months. I'm in total disbelief. To me, this instantly made me realize my family and I have to learn to make sacrifices.

On the top of the list are my eating habits. In this chapter I want you to look at your list as well. My list is as follows, containing things or stuff I can do better at buying or spending:

1. Food: I eat out for lunch pretty much five days a week when I work. That is roughly ten to fifteen dollars a day—not to mention I have a family, and at least three days out the week we eat out. That's a minimum at twenty-five dollars each night we eat fast food.

2. Shoes/clothes: For some reason, I have been addicted to shoes and clothes since I was about twelve. Fashion is definitely a passion of mine, and one day I'll make millions of it—just watch.

My problem is now that I have a daughter shes consistently growing, so I have to make sure she has clothes and shoes (SHE'S GROWING).

3. My business venture cost: As I was talking to a friend who is also a business owner, we both realized it takes money to make money. I can do better at budgeting how I am going to spend the money for my business instead of being so random.

Those are my main three things that I can make sacrifices in to do better and manage my way into the success that says my bank account can allow me to do whatever. Success to me is being fully proud of where I am in life. I'm working on that success. The end goal through this process is to find my purpose, recreate my drive, and figure out my true passion that will lead to my success, as well as guiding you on your way to your success. I am good at a lot of things, but what will I be known for?

What's your list?

1. ______________________________

2. ______________________________

3. ______________________________

Day 4

LETDOWNS

Thus far we have discussed focus, discipline, and sacrifice. Today I want to discuss letdowns._To be let down is to find yourself in a place where you thought you had a plan or had a map you started on with great intentions, hopes, and dreams, then *boom*! Curveball called life! Nothing is going as planned; you're stuck at a crossroads.

For instance, I started my business, Style Inc., a clothing line and boutique for women with select men's T-shirt/hoodies. I was (and still am in some ways) in the process of really getting this off the ground. I went and got my license, made the clothing, purchased from vendors, started making the website, etc., had my Instagram friends getting excited actually, buying things—you know, a little support. Every week I'm buying stuff, putting in the work, but not a whole lot because the money I was bringing in I spent right back out, being motivated, trying to grind it out.

To this day I'm still trying to figure out the next moves for Style Inc. It's a letdown to know it hasn't met its full potential. Have I given up? Definitely not at all! What I did was think of another lane to cross over into. We started a YouTube channel—granted, it is also hard work! Four women with kids and busy lives can get very hectic. If you're reading this, go like and subscribe to our channel, Sh*ddd Let's Talk. In my mind, switching over into this lane will allow me to grasp a new audience.

By grasping an audience, I can wear my T-shirts or clothing, and that can spark a new following. Also, it gives me another platform to promote my ventures. I'm always plugging something I'm doing because in my heart I am the one in my family who is going to break the generational curses. I carry everything on my shoulders because I know it's something special in me. I can't describe it other than it is in my gut. I am not searching for fame; I want the success. My motivation behind all this is the success. I know I get let down a lot, but I also know if I keep going that the lessons were all in the letdown.

Currently at my job I am second in command. I have been itching to be first in command for some time, but while writing I am discovering my focus has been off. I lack the discipline, haven't made the necessary sacrifices, and tend to dwell on my letdowns. Once I get on track with the four things I have previously discussed, my only way is up.

Here is another exercise. Write down or talk about the things you may not have discussed with anyone. Get them out now because after this you or I will no longer look back on our letdowns. Letdowns and losses are all the lessons you need to prevail in your success plan.

My letdowns:

- Not becoming a general manager when I am doing the job
- Not graduating on time
- Not saving to buy a house sooner
- Learning how to budget late
- Letting myself down when I settle for mediocrity

What's on your mind?

____

____

____

____

Day 5

PROGRESS

Yesterday we discussed letdowns, so in alternation I want to talk about progress. The definition of progress is forward or onward movement toward a destination. This past week I had a move out of my apartment—me, a procrastinator, someone whose focus is off, and who lacks time management. I needed to be out of my apartment by Saturday. I started packing on Thursday.

In one day I cleared out a whole room by myself. My vision was clear: it was about the progress. I was happy because I stood in the room that was clear, not in any other room. It was the progress of what I could see, not what I couldn't.

I tend to get down on myself when I look at everyone around me. I have to remember where I come from. Although I am the director of a hotel now, I can still remember when I was cleaning twenty rooms a day. I can remember trying to figure out where I was going and what I was actually doing.

Progress will come over time, but one thing you have to do is look at where you started, the in-between time and where you are now. Take a look at my progress. I want you to look at your timeline of progression as well.

Housekeeper: director of rooms

Hated school in the eleventh grade (I was going through some things)

Graduated college twice

Poetry writer: writing a book

Didn't want to listen to authority; became an authority figure over 115 employees

Started at $6.40 but now moved to an upper middle-class salary

My list of progress isn't too long, but it does show how the things that I have endured allowed me to be where I am now. Progress! I have failed way more times than I have yet to succeed; it's the progress within the journey.

This exercise has taught me that the journey has not been easy at all, but it allows me to see that I've been taking the necessary steps to get where I am going. I made progress that I am very proud of. Can you look back and say the same? I am very sure that you will be surprised at how far you have come.

Embrace the progress. Although it is great to embrace your progress, just make sure you don't get comfortable; the work isn't done. Everything attached to being successful is about taking steps—baby steps or full-blown leaps. All will come with work and day-to-day efforts to get to the next level. That is why it's called progress.

Looking at your timeline allows you to create new habits, consider progression as a curving road. It is not a straight shot to success. It may include setbacks, letdowns, two steps forward and then one step back. Everyone's progress timeline is different. The importance of the timeline is to see where you started and where you are now, so that it is used as motivation to keep going.

What did you learn looking at your progress timeline?

____

____

____

Day 6

COMFORT

Through the journey you and only you can decide your end result. Let's say you've gotten the house, the car or cars you want. Are you then considered successful? Success and comfort are like oil and water; they will never mix.

Day five we broke down progress in the terms of seeing things happen but not getting so comfortable in the progress that you forget that there is a goal to achieve. I talked about clearing out one room during my packing and moving stage. I made progress, but I couldn't get comfortable with one room when the apartment was a two-bedroom, two full baths, kitchen, dining room, and a living room. Progress but not comfort.

There have been days where I have wanted to give up becoming my definition of success, but usually when I am at a low point mentally, I try to put my head down and just work. How do I work? Paper and pen are my favorite. I have to organize my thoughts over and over again. In order for me to make changes and create new habits, it is imperative to keep my thoughts intact. If I have to regain focus, find ways to discipline myself, or figure out the sacrifices I need to make, it can't get done with a bogged-down mind. Writing things down allows one to solve problems and empty the brain of useless information. What are some things you have become comfortable with?

For me it has been life. I have struggled to grind how I used to. When you begin to eat more often than you starve, it's a lot easier to become complacent. In reality, I'm still just getting by, but these are the real conversations I want you to have with yourself. Are you living, or are you getting by?

Most people who are really getting to it and are successful are really out here living life. I mean living their Lil Duval best life. I remember being so hungry when I made a lot less money and I was in college working two jobs. I worked at Walmart and Kmart, and now it's in my mind that working two jobs is just too much work. I have side hustles that do not require a lot of thought or work, but to work an actual full-time job and part-time job I'd probably die! Lol, not literally, but this is how I know that I am at a level of comfort that I need to come out of. My success will derive from the work I am willing to put in.

When I was really hungry to make it, I was going to cosmetology school, had a full-time job. There were days I would wake up at 5:00 a.m., do hair, get ready for work as a housekeeper, clean sixteen to twenty rooms, and be off work by 4:00 p.m., just to make sure I was at school by 5:00 p.m. Then, I would leave there at 10:00 p.m. and head home. After that long day, a lot of times I would still take hair appointments after school. I went to work and school five days out of the week and took appointments three or four days out of the week because I was determined to make more than $8.50.

Fast forward to now, where I am making way more than $8.50 an hour, I'm hungry, but my drive has slowed down, and that is where I am itching to get back to. Of course, the goal is not to work hard forever, but to work hard right now, so that later I will have enough money saved and put back to enjoy life.

When we decide to come out of our comfort zone, it can mean one more unlocked door through the hallway of success. We now know that we must take back our focus, obtain a level of discipline that we have yet to push ourselves to, make many changes, and STOP BEING COMFORTABLE!

What have you gotten comfortable with?

____

____

____

____

____

____

____

What did you learn from day six about yourself?

____

____

____

____

____

____

____

____

Day 7

SEPARATION/ISOLATION

Separate: Divide or cause to divide to constituent or distinct elements. Isolate: To be or remain alone or apart from others. This topic may cause you to identify people, places, or things that are causing you not to reach your full level of purpose and/or success.

When I was thinking of becoming more than a housekeeper, I learned that I was a part of the problem-child group. Although I worked very hard at my job and cleaned better than any of the other housekeepers, I failed at keeping my mouth shut. I was usually the one who spoke up about anything and everything, so I stuck out like a sore thumb. In my mind, right is right and wrong is wrong, and when I was younger, I had to let it be known exactly how I felt and what needed to be changed. Around age twenty-five, I evolved into a more observant individual rather than the quick-to-speak individual.

It is OK to speak your mind, but you also have to know that there is a time and a place for everything. It is OK to advocate for the things that are righteous, but you also have to watch the people who are asking you to stick your neck out for the cause but won't stand on the front line with you. Beware of those kinds of people because nine times out of ten they are achieving goals quietly and allowing you to look like a fool with no sense of direction.

When I began to sort out where I wanted to be in life, I noticed I needed to change my surroundings. I kept telling myself: *I do not want to be a housekeeper for the rest of my life.* I searched for a new position within the hotel. My now mentor posted that the Courtyard was in need of a front desk employee and a barista, so I messaged her on Facebook—we worked at another property prior to the job posting.

At the time of me making changes to where I was, I realized I needed to separate myself from my surroundings. If I hadn't, I would've probably been fired because I was already labeled as one of the problematic employees. Separation is not bad when you are obtaining goals. You may have to separate from people, places, and negative energy. Separate from social media. Separating yourself from people may be the toughest one to endure.

At times we tend to think that because a person has been around for a while that it won't harm us to take them on our journey. Wrong! We are all human, and in being human we can have tunnel vision and not see everything around us. When there are people around you who start saying things like "You changing on me," "You don't hang out like we use to," "You think you doing something because you got a new job, a promotion, a house, a new car" (anything that they don't have), these are all phrases to be aware of. As you get older your wants and needs will definitely change, especially if you go from not having a child or children to having all of the above. Your life changes drastically, so within these changes the need to succeed becomes more of a necessity.

People who criticize you for going after your goals are like leeches; they want to suck all of the aspiration out of you so that it seems like you and they are on the same level. Get away from people sucking the life out of you. You need brainstormers, creators, visionaries, influencers, and pushers around you. I thrive off of seeing other people getting to a bag; it makes me sit down and get focused on myself.

All places aren't good places. Just because you are used to the environment doesn't mean it's best for you. I find myself being more creative when I take myself out of my normal element. I think clearer; I see things I never thought of. Your surroundings can be detrimental to your success. Be an explorer of all things even if you don't like certain things. Explore first then decide if it's not for you. Take yourself out of your norm. You will be amazed at the difference it can make in your life.

Negative energy: I cannot say this enough, but we tend to think we are superheroes who can stay around negativity and not attract it. This, my friend, is a lie. If you lay in dirt you will get dirty. If you surround yourself with negativity you, my friend, will become the poster child for negativity. In order to elevate you must separate. Isolate yourself from these things for a while, such as social media. Social media can be a gift and a curse, but if you don't learn to shut it off it, will be more of a curse than gift. Become one with your journey, eliminate outside noise, hear your thoughts. How do you find your direction if you never turn off the noise of the world around you?

What is it that you need to separate from?

____

____

____

____

____

____

When was the last time you went into isolation?

____

____

____

____

____

____

Day 8
DETERMINATION

Determination is a positive emotional feeling that involves persevering toward a difficult goal in spite of obstacles. Determination occurs prior to goal attainment and serves to motivate behavior that will help achieve one's goal. This is the Wikipedia definition via Google. For me, the will to get up every day with determination in your heart is a personal character trait. Not everyone has the will or the want to get up and continue on a journey. What are you willing to do to succeed?

I recently shared a video of Kevin Hart, and he put determination together so well. Kevin said, "It's easy to give up, but what's hard is going hard after you've gotten nothing from it, after working as hard as you could, yet get up another day and give another 100 percent. That's a real grind: to get up every day and continuously push yourself." When you're being recognized for the work you've put in it makes it so much easier to be motivated, but when people keep going after no one has recognized their efforts, it takes a strong individual. That is what true determination looks like.

This can be the hardest thing to ever do, but the person who can take this in stride and keep pushing has no choice other than to succeed. I know I am determined to succeed because I constantly reinvent myself over and over again. In the face of every letdown, I sucked it up and kept going—still going, still trying. I push through every failed attempt.

Being determined can make or break you; only you can decide how successful you become. I have been discouraged and let down more times than I can write or remember in this book, yet I have refused to give up. If I give up what message will I send to the people who depend on me? Be determined enough to leave a legacy behind.

The thing that has helped me the most is mapping out my progress timeline. It has allowed me to visually look at my wins, take from them, and add to the progress. Progress can be reassurance that you are moving in the right direction. Throughout this process of me finding my path to my success and you finding yours, we get to look at our journey and the process that it is taking us through. A lot of times people can tell you all they've been through, but they never took the time out for themselves to really analyze their then to now, which could be used for so much more motivation.

I want to meet my full potential. I am sure you would like to as well. It does not matter how many times I get knocked down. If I'm knocked down twenty times, I will get up twenty-one times. You have to make it up in your mind that you are here to win. I promise myself to wake up every day with determination in my heart.

Have you been determined to do better?

____

____

____

____

What hope have you lost and why?

____

____

____

____

Can you get knocked down and get back up?

____

____

____

____

Day 9

F.E.A.R

Fear can motivate you, or fear can stop you; it is up to the individual. Every time I have stepped into a higher position it came with fear—fear that I wouldn't do my best or that I'd get too comfortable and not want more out of life. Fear of not succeeding has always made me strive for everything, but fear has also held me back from getting what I feel like I deserve.

There have been so many positions that I knew I was qualified for—or maybe even over qualified for—that I psyched myself out and said, "Why would they give me that job?" Do not ever second guess your ability. Don't get me wrong: the same fear that drove me away from different opportunities has led me to where I am today. I remember a twenty-four-year-old me being a supervisor for Marriott Hotel chain, just starting my career upon getting my first supervisor role. I remember being so excited because I knew I knew the job. The night before I began this journey, I became so nervous, so scared. I called my great friend and mentor Markisha Gates, telling her how scared I had become and overwhelmed—just that quick after my excitement wore off. Markisha's exact words to me were, "Jamie, you know the job. Go in there and do exactly what you know how to do."

Those words stuck with me. To this day, seven years later, I try my best not to be fearful of anything because you can go into any situation doing exactly what you know how to do then learn along the way. I can say that I have experienced being nervous, or my anxiety may kick in, but I will never live in fear. I allow the little bit of fear to motivate how I move into my next journey I'm so scared of not becoming; that is the only thing I fear. Never be so fearful that you won't try. If you continue to scare yourself out of things how are you to realize what lies ahead, or how are you to reach your full potential? Do not fear yourself out of success.

F - Face
E - Everything
A - and
R - Rise

Identify your fears.

____

____

____

____

____

____

What have to not accomplished because of fear?

____

____

____

____

____

____

Day 10

HARD WORK

After day nine, I decided to dive deeper into thought because I discussed fear. Yes, I've been fearful at times, but one thing about me is I have never been fearful of hard work. I truly believe that even though I lack focus at times, by beginning to restructure my discipline and creating routines for myself I am seeing that even though I may not have a strong connection to each word, I realize the ability I have when it comes to working hard. It has gotten me a long way. Hard work is going the extra mile even when you think you are near the end.

When I was a housekeeper getting a sixteen- to twenty-room board to complete, I'd listen to all my coworkers nag and complain about the work we were given, but I'd look at it as a challenge. Challenges have always ignited something in me. Me accomplishing something daily made a beast out of me. It's like it doesn't matter what has been placed in front me because I know I will out work any of my competition on any given day due to my will.

Today I sit here and think of the success story I am trying to make. I feel as though I have worked very hard on my journey, but I do know that there is more in me; otherwise, I would have reached my destination by this point. What do I need to work harder on? I think I can do more with everything that I have placed on my plate—Style Inc., Sh*ddd Let's Talk, my writing and creative thinking process, my job. In order to get to my next level I have to push myself harder. You have to be willing to push yourself harder. I have no limitations on myself, which is a good thing. Never place yourself in a box because you will limit your ability to achieve.

I have three sisters. One day, I was talking to my youngest sister, and she asked me: if I could do one thing and I knew I would not fail at it, what would it be? She then said, "You are good at so many things." It instantly made me think this may be true, but honestly, I choose to work very hard on anything and everything that comes my way. I was told do not do anything that you are not willing to put 100 percent into because it will not be the best representation of you and your brand. We as people have to look at ourselves as a built brand already and stand on the representation of ourselves.

I'm allowing this to sink in. I'm good at a lot of things, but what am I great at? Honestly, I'm not sure if I actually know the answer to this question yet, but I am destined to find out. However, I can answer her initial question. If I could do anything and know that it would not fail, it would be fashion and writing, making people remember my words. I think this is why I love rap music so much—artists' words take me places that I didn't realize they could. Fashion, to me, is a form of expression, and I am so intrigued by that interpretation of art. I get a high off my friends and family calling me to help put pieces together. When I create my hoodies and T-shirts, it allows me to be in a happy place I didn't know existed for me. My only issue with this is that it is not paying my bills at the moment. This is where my hard work and determination will place me where I would like to be within my success story. I have to work harder on Style Inc. I have to work harder on this book so my words may inspire the world or an up-and-coming generation. Words never die; they live forever.

> "There are no secrets to success. It is the result of preparation, hard work, and learning from failure." —Colin Powell

> "Everybody wants to be famous, but nobody wants to do the work. I live by that. You grind so you can play hard. At the end of the day, you put all the work in, and eventually it will pay off. It could be in a year; it could be in thirty years. Eventually your hard work will pay off." —Kevin Hart

What can you work harder on?

Have you given up because you haven't seen your hard work visually?

Day 11

OBSTACLES

It seems like every time I turn around I'm faced with an obstacle to overcome. Whether it is making decisions on changing my shift or being able to spend time with my daughter, I feel it is all a part of the many obstacles you may face before you reach a certain level of success.

On a day where I was absolutely going through hell, I kept asking myself: *Why am I faced with so many challenges throughout my career when I work hard?* I try to follow the rules, but the ones that are making the money are the ones that don't follow any rules. I'm here to tell you I know it's only part of my journey. Every incident that has come my way I stayed ten toes down, praying though it all, and came out victorious in every one.

Success comes with obstacles. Obstacles are the hurdles you find yourself jumping over daily. Here are a few I'm constantly faced with:

- Being a strong-minded black woman
- Being younger than most in my field
- Being a woman in a male-dominated industry
- Being a mother with a career

I challenge you to write yours down as well.

___

___

___

___

___

___

___

___

___

___

___

I face my obstacles by taking the good with the bad. I have stayed calm in the presence of those who try to break me. I am currently on a twenty-day fast—no meat, and no sodas or juice, only water. I am four days in, but I hope it will help me gain clarity of a lot of the obstacles I've faced.

I know greatness is placed on my life through this journaling. I know I should gain clarity. As for you reading this and figuring things out with me, I hope you put things into perspective as well, and you figure out your next venture. Obstacles will definitely thrive while you're on the journey to success.

Day 12

PATIENCE

How is your ability to wait? I've never been great at waiting, but everything is a process. Lately I've been hearing people—especially rapper Jezzy—talk about trusting the process. It is hard to do, trust me. I know it all too well.

If you are anything like me, you can't see the forest for the trees, meaning it is hard to know success lies behind a few doors that are unopened, but in reality, you won't be worried about the opened doors; you tend to stay focused on the door you are currently standing behind. The key to it is it only takes faith the size of a mustard seed to believe and achieve. For example, I have a two year old, and watching her develop I've learned I have to trust the process. As soon as she turned two I was expecting her to talk and it to be easy to potty train her. Man, I was wrong! Kourtylnn (my daughter) did not start talking until December. My daughter will be three in May. She gets on the pot when she wants to. I tell myself, "It's all in the process."

This success thing isn't easy at all, but you will definitely be thrown off your course if you don't realize the scarifies, obstacles, fears, and lots of other things that can deter you from your path of success. Patience is a major key to success because there will lie many obstacles in front of your journey. Patience gives you a chance to step back and reset. If everything you do you rush, you will make way more mistakes than necessary. Again, you have to understand everything in life is a process.

Have you ever heard the phrase, "If one door hasn't opened, I will praise my higher being in the hallway"? This term refers to your attitude in your willingness to wait. A lot of times, we miss out on better because we become tired of waiting. I know I did this multiple times when I was in search of a new job. The worst place I worked at was an Embassy Suites. I won't say where it is, but I found it to be terrible because it had no solid foundation, and the owners did not want to put the necessary money back into the building, which made it even more difficult for me to do my job. It was my fault that I even took a job there. I was rushing, wanting to be closer to my daughter, and that clouded my judgment as to the right environment I wanted to place myself in. I know that there's no mistakes made when God places certain things in your path, but I do know that we humans can make bad choices because we are rushing.

Lately, I have been getting better at praying about things before I make a bad decision. I remember sending my pastor a direct message (shout-out to Pastor Mike McClure, Jr.) because everything at my job was going wrong, and I was ready to jump out the window in my decision-making process. He said, "Before you fly off the handle, we pray and allow God to lead us in the right direction." I am not an expert at this, but I am learning and trying to be a lot better at being obedient. He was absolutely correct. I was patient enough to do the work and be patient through the process. Had I not, I probably would've quit my job at the wrong time. It is OK to seek help and rational answers from the people around you. This is why I said that you have to surround yourself with the right people and energy. What if I had called or inboxed a person who lacked patience and was not rational enough to view my situation in a different light? As you grow in your journey, you will realize that patience will keep you from making decisions you may regret later.

Patience: the capacity to accept or tolerate delay, trouble, or suffering without getting angry or upset. Remember, how you wait during your process could determine the outcome. It's OK to get frustrated here and there, but remember, it's a part of the process. We cannot lose if we are making the necessary changes and handling things accordingly.

What has patience taught you?

What could be different in your life had you waited a little while longer?

Day 13

100 NOS + 1 YES!!!

When you water a seed, you expect it to grow, but if there is no rain for your seeds, do you give up on your harvest or the way you feed your family? No! Instead you remind yourself that no rain now doesn't mean no rain later. My harvest might grow in time to sell and make my money to feed my family. So, let's talk about the nos and the yes.

The nos are discouraging, without a doubt, but it comes with patience, as we talked about on day twelve. What have you done when you were hoping and wishing, even praying, yes? What do you take away from the no? To me, no only means "not yet." Someone else's timing isn't your timing.

There comes a point in time where you look at everyone around you and think: *What am I doing compared to those around me?* One thing I've said to my friends: this younger generation has figured it out early. Finding your passion and purpose early on has to be a great feeling. For those of us who haven't figured it out yet, we still have time. Do not get discouraged. I changed my mind so many times about what I wanted to become. I wanted to be a teacher; I wanted to be a psychologist (I am infatuated with the thought of how we think differently). I wanted to be a hairstylist—stylist to celebrities—and a motivational speaker. I turned out to be a director in the hospitality industry. One hundred nos and one yes. No, I didn't become a physiologist; no, I didn't become a hairstylist, etc., but yes, I have been able to get in the minds of people I worked with to help them in their situations. I have motivated and encouraged a few people to conquer their goals and their dreams.

No doesn't mean you should stop. It simply means be patient, reevaluate, and keep pushing. I believe in being pushed into your destiny if you want it bad enough. If you believe in the universe aligning with destiny, all things you're dreaming of will manifest. This means you also believe that a no is sent to place you in your correct position. It is like a no is placed in your direction to steer your wheel correctly when you have no GPS through life. One hundred nos will never be sent to destroy you, but one yes could change your whole life in the matter of an instance.

Think about what nos you may have received, and then the perfect yes came directly after. My example is: I remember being left at a property (hotel) after my first year of being a supervisor and accomplishing the number-one ranking Courtyard Marriott Hotel in Alabama—a huge deal for me at twenty-four years old. Then the GM that believed in me left. I tried my best to think positively because the new guy seemed alright. He had credentials behind him, a clean-cut look like he had it all together. Boy, was I completely wrong. In my supervisor role, I also started training and teaching myself to become an operational manager. In my mind it would be easy: I knew the property. I trained and worked hard for it, so I deserved it, right? Wrong again! This new GM did not like me at all. I battled with him several times over him trying to destroy my character. Thank God there were a few people who knew of my hard work and dedication around the city of Birmingham, so he couldn't destroy what I'd built.

I remember having a phone conversation with him where he lied and told me he was interested in me taking the position as the operations manager. He said he would interview me for the job, etc., but a few days later I learned that they gave it to someone else, a person who I trained—but that's another story for another day. Be careful with people—that is all I'm going to say about that.

Anyway, I had to regain perspective and reposition myself. In doing so I received a call from my previous GM, asking if I wanted to move to Charlotte, North Carolina, for a job. It was a lateral move but more money, my vision was to elevate myself at this new property but also questioning myself. I had no money saved other than a 401K I started at nineteen or twenty. I'd never been to Charlotte, yet there was an opportunity sitting right in front of me. I initially was anxious about doing something out of my norm. I was ready to turn the job down and say no because I said to myself, "How could I move with no money saved or any way to get ahold of some right then and there?" My lease wasn't up until February. It was November.

It wasn't until I had a conversation with someone (I can't remember who) and they said to me, "If you don't go you could regret it for the rest of your life." Turns out it did change my life. I lived in Charlotte for exactly one year. Within that year I met my fiancé, so I feel like that yes that I did get put me on the path to my success, and I'm so grateful for that one yes as well as the no. I learned that through that process, my attitude was firm on my beliefs of right and wrong, yet I did what I was supposed to and my patience and attitude determined my altitude.

Day 14

ATTITUDE

Have you ever heard that your attitude can determine your altitude? I'll be honest; I'm conflicted with this because I've been in several situations where I was being done wrong by managers. At times it made me upset because I had to fight for what was right. I don't like being fired up, but I am a person who will go to the end of the end when I know I am in the right. I will tell anyone who is on the road to success that you have to beware of people in your path sent to destroy your path to success. There is an old saying that churchgoers, such as myself, go by: If God hasn't opened the door yet, praise him in the hallway. This refers to your attitude while you wait.

Story time: I can think back to me wanting the iPhone 11. Well, I couldn't get a new phone until December 28, 2019. I waited my time. So, it's December 28 and I'm in the Verizon store. I specifically told the agent I wanted the iPhone 11 Pro Max. Well, I was given an iPhone 11—not the Max. I kept thinking it was small but didn't think much of it. The next day I went to Five Below (great store, by the way) to buy a phone case. I tell the cashier what I was looking for, and she said, "You have the iPhone 11, not the 11 Pro Max." So the cashier proceeded to tell me the differences.

I went to work that day, and when I got off work, I went by Verizon. This is where I was tested. I see the guy who sold me the wrong phone, and I say to him, "Hey, I asked for the iPhone 11 Pro Max and you gave me the 11."

He immediately goes into defense mode and says, "No, I gave you what you asked for."

I say, "No, but I'm not here to argue. I just want the phone I asked for."

He says, "Well, there's going to be a fifty-dollar restocking fee as well as another 100 dollars because of the price of the phone."

I take a deep breath and say, "I paid you 55 dollars yesterday. So you mean to tell me I'm going to pay over 200 for a phone now?"

As I waited there patiently, I told him that I didn't understand how I would pay this amount now, but I wanted what I wanted. He said, "Let me check a few things out for you."

I waited a little while longer. He finally came back and said, "I will only need the restocking fee since the phone has been open."

I looked at him and said, "I guess it's true your attitude can determine your altitude."

He said, "You are absolutely right because the guy standing over there? Their attitude is awful, and I'm not interested in helping him in the manner in which he was asking because of the attitude he has given me since he arrived in the store." He also told me he had something to help keep my AirPods sitting in my ears since I had issues keeping them in my ears.

I told him, "Thank you, and I understand how frustrating it can be in customer service."

Much like the story, it's the same thing when it comes to succeeding in life. While you wait on what you are believing in or hoping for, your attitude shall determine how far you get in life.

How has your attitude been during your season of waiting?

____

____

____

____

Can you rearrange your attitude toward some things?

___

___

___

___

___

Day 15

OBEDIENCE

The ability to follow instructions. Success is associated with how you are able to take commands as well. I truly believe in order to lead you must be able to follow. Someone who has come before you can definitely give you the tools to properly navigate through your career, or just in your life in general. Obedience is defined with compliance: with an order, request, or law, or submission to another's authority. Obedience can put you in a make-or-break situation because in every situation you have to know when to be the teacher and when to be the student.

Just because someone takes a different approach to obtaining a goal doesn't mean they don't have the necessary tools to get you where you want to be. Many times, we have breakdowns in our lives when we have missed, disobeyed, or disregarded an instruction. Have you ever forgotten just "one" ingredient in your favorite recipe and it didn't come out right? Well, that is the same with obedience. In order to have the correct finished product, you have to make sure you follow the recipe. This is something that I struggle with a lot because everybody always wants to be right or be the "leader" in a sense, but sometimes you have to take the backseat until it's your turn to steer the ship.

True obedience governs our thoughts, our relationships, and all our actions. True obedience is tested and proved through hard times, and trust me, I know hard times. I try to not let those bad days affect the path that I'm on or affect anyone around me because sometimes your disobedience can rub off on a peer who looks up to you.

As we discussed, it is important to not feed on negative energy. I try to commit and be obedient in all entities of my life, from my spirituality, well-being, career, and raising my daughter. In order for all of these natures in life to come together in the end, in order to have a certain level of success, you must be obedient.

What have you not been obedient with?

____

____

____

____

____

____

____

What do you keep ignoring, but it constantly occupies your mind?

____

____

____

____

____

____

____

Day 16

REFLECTION AFTER THE FIRST FIFTEEN DAYS

There have been a few things I've changed after being on my journey. I've learned that allowing myself to change one negative into a positive allows me to continue making positive strides toward my purpose, my passion, and what I deem to be successful. I have definitely worked on my time management. This has helped me structure my days a lot better, for me to make more time for my passion so I can figure out my purpose. I did start getting clothes ready on Sunday and, OMG, who knew? I should've been doing this a long time ago.

Sacrifices I've made have been cutting back on bad spending habits. I started back grocery shopping and making a list for me. It may not seem like much to you, but it's everything to me. At work I emailed a new schedule for myself that allows me to monitor both departments that are under me within the week, as well as lets me be able and sit down with my managers to help them move forward.

After you've read this, I want you to sit and reflect as well. What changes have you made to help you toward your success journey, and how have they helped you?

We have fourteen days left. By day thirty-one I want us to have placed all of our lives in perspective, make affective change, and be well on our way to passion and purpose. I truly believe that one who is truly successful is one who is living in their purpose and is truly happy. That is definitely a big part of success: being able to do what you love and gain monetary value while doing so.

Day 17

PASSION

Do you know your passion and what you truly love to do? Can you make money from your passion? You may be like me and have many things you are great at but fail to pick a thing that will allow you to be successful. Is there anything you truly love to do? Can you make money from your passion? You may be like me and have many things you are great at but fail to pick a thing that will allow you to be successful.

I repeated these sentences because we do not ask ourselves these questions enough. We do not let questions like this to sit in our brain until we can fully answer them. Even with passion you will still have to work hard, not get comfortable, stay focused, and be obedient as well as be patient. The need for success should be driven with passion. If we all did what we loved, the world would be an absolutely better place.

Lately I've been asking myself, "What am I really passionate about?" It won't be easy to find your passion because you may overlook a few things, or overlook what you love because you never thought of it bringing you success. I suggest once you find said passion do your research. There may be several ways to bring your passion to an audience. The things I find myself being passionate about I will list, and you should list yours as well. It helps a lot to write things down, to see your vision manifest, but remember, it is a process and you have to trust your process.

I suggest asking yourself: Is this a hobby, or can it be profitable? Have I perfected my craft? Is there a need for it in the market? Do I know of someone who could help me? Do I have the resources? Have I brainstormed? Am I prepared for the journey of ups and downs?

More importantly, two things I will say: make sure you keep your job, whatever it is, or at least keep a source of income to fund your passion.

Last but not least—and it is probably one of the most important things I will ever tell you through this journey—never, I mean never, ever, no matter how many times you put it down and pick it back up, never give up.

Ways to tap into your passion:

1. Find out what makes you happy.
2. Identify what you can do with ease.
3. Identify your weaknesses.
4. Identify your strengths.
5. Ask others what you excel, at from their perspective.
6. Use these answers and connect the dots.

My Passions List:

- Helping people
- Teaching people
- Being happy with in life
- The process of thought
- Art
- Fashion
- Writing to express myself

- Motivationally speaking to people
- Traveling
- History
- Wealth

What's your passion?

____

____

____

____

____

____

____

____

____

____

____

____

____

Day 18

RESEARCH

Day seventeen we discussed passion and went on to talk about researching your passion to figure out a few things. Research is very important if you are going to become successful. Google is great, and a mentor is even better. There isn't much new under the sun; more than likely, whatever it is you want to do has been done, or there is someone with the same idea. If by chance you come across that person who has the same passions or ideas, try to collaborate. They say two heads are better than one. There isn't anything wrong with being successful with someone you trust. Just remember to set ground rules; always be open minded when it comes to binding contracts (please read everything before you sign it), as well as non-disclosure agreements even non-compete clauses. In all aspects of becoming successful, protect your biggest assets, which are yourself and your creativeness.

Someone who really wants to be successful will understand the business aspect of collaborating with another person. Research other companies or people who are doing what you want to do. Study the industry. Perfect the down sides. Researching will allow you to go into your situation without blinders. I still don't have a title for this book, but I have already looked up the bestselling self-help books in year 2019. I studied the way they looked, the covers, the topics—all of that I believe will help me. I know I want to catch the attention of my readers. My pastor has a phrase he's used and stated: "It's OK to be a copy cat, as long as you got the right cat to copy."

Knowledge is power, knowledge can also determine how, when, and why you will win in the end. Think about school. If you break it down, most of the time spent going to school we are asked to do papers—research this; tell me about that. I can admit there are a lot of unnecessary things taught in school, but researching is not one of them. Reading and being able to comprehend what you read is a gateway to success. I think the reason why they asked us for papers on this and that is because they were teaching us to learn about your craft, know what came before you, identify differences. It is right in front of us; we just have to be readily available to research it. Do not be afraid to be a student before you become the teacher.

Before I became a director in the hospitality industry, I remember studying all my supervisors and managers I had. I studied the negative as well as the positive. In anything you do, study the negative and the positive, then prefect it. If you can create positives from negatives, then your outcome should be far greater.

What do you need to research?

____

____

____

____

What have you been thinking about that will make you successful?

____

____

____

____

Day 19

PREPARATIONS

If you stay ready, you don't have to get ready. Think about it: If you don't prepare for opportunities, how will you take full advantage of them? One way I say being prepared will help you: if you have done research, then it prepares you to speak on your passion or purpose. I tell people all the time, "You never know who you may meet that has the key to your future." Being knowledgeable and prepared to speak to those things will help you. The late, great Nipsey said, "Luck is just being prepared at all times, so when the door opens, you're ready."

Have you prepared for your success? If so, how? Being prepared prevents errors. It allows people to see that you know exactly what you are doing. What can you do that you have yet to do that will stand out from everyone else? Prepared I am not maybe the reason I have not. This was a short insert, but I want you to reflect on being prepared and preparing for the success you are expecting. Have you practiced being in boardrooms? Have you practiced making life-changing decisions? When you are preparing to change lives around you, you have to stay ready. Prepare for the good and the bad.

Day 20

MANIFESTING

Learn to speak things into existence. Speak things that are not as though they were. Have you done a vision board? With vision boards it's OK to do them by year. Last year when I did a vision board, I sectioned things off so that I could categorize my goals for my career, family, and travel plans, as well as a prayer for those things. I am a spiritual person, so this helps me with my beliefs. If you are not, you still have to truly believe in your ability. Imagine being in front of people who have the ability to help your dreams come true. How can you make someone else believe in whatever you want to bring to life if you don't even believe it yourself?

In order to manifest your beliefs, you need to be very precise about what you want. You have to know exactly what you want, whether it's a job or your own business. Speak what you would like to make. It may sound crazy, but in every building I've received a job in, I've walked through the halls, praying or manifesting my hopes of what I wanted to happen—most of which I did manifest into existence.

Write things down. I really believe in writing down hopes, dreams, or ambition goals. Write it down, over and over again.

Free your mind of the negative thoughts of why you can't have whatever you want to manifest into your destiny. Mental blocks will allow you to defeat yourself. The only person who can stop you is you. What is for you is for you. If something passed you, then it was never for you, or it isn't the time for it. It doesn't happen overnight, so you will need to be patient.

Can you visualize what you want? Place yourself there. In order to manifest the success you speak of, you must be able to see it, hear it, taste it. Consistency is the key.

What do you really want?

____

____

____

____

How much do you want to make?

____

____

____

____

____

What actions have you taken toward this?

____

____

____

____

Can you see it?

____

____

____

____

____

Day 21

BUDGETING

Budget: a financial plan for a defined period—a one-year accomplishment, a five-year accomplishment, a ten-year accomplishment. I truly believe you can budget your way into success. Have I accomplished this aspect yet? No. Have I made better life choices to get on track? Yes.

As I've been writing I'm definitely taking my own advice. I wrote down all my bills and saw where there was room from improvement. Even a better perspective: someone I grew up with has a better way of putting things into perspective when it comes to budgeting. He calls it Crush Thirty. How ironic that I'm writing this in reference to becoming successful after age thirty. Let's do this Crush Thirty. I'll put an example here, but you can also check him out via Instagram: Chad Black (@ blackychad).

In this exercise you will need all your bills—even Apple subscribers or Google Play for you Android users. (Note: these are not my bills, but an example.)

Crush	30
Rent $1,000 /	30 = $33.33
Phone bill $100 /	30 = $3.33
Car note $350 /	30 = $11.66
Car insurance $150 /	30 = $2.00
Apple subscription $40 /	30 = $1.33
Day care $400 /	30= $13.33
Household Supplies $200 /	30 = $6.66
Miscellaneous $200 /	30 = $6.67
	Total = 78.31 to make this daily

You will need to make $78.31 daily in order to live your life, but the keys are if you make $10.00 an hour with forty hours a week, at eight hours a day you are making $80 dollars a day—no taxes being taken out—that only leaves $1.69. The trick is: your job will only require a full-time position to work eight hours a day for five days a week. You do not get a day off from paying bills; therefore, a lot of us are robbing Peter to pay Paul. If you cannot look at your bills and say what you make daily outweighs the bills you make daily, it is time to cancel some subscriptions, rethink where you live, and cut back on the unnecessary things.

What does your Crush Thirty tell you?

____

____

____

____

____

List all your subscriptions. Do you really need these?

Day 22

GRATITUDE/ THANKFULNESS

In each step toward your success, have you reflected and been thankful for where you were and where you are now? If you haven't been, then that may be the problem. Being thankful can take you a long way. I've learned to be just as grateful for the bad as I've been for the good things I've encountered in life.

"People who are grateful not only seek out more success, they draw success into their lives," Erika Andersen stated in *a Forbes* article entitled "How Feeling Grateful Can Make You More Successful." There have been many studies that have shown that practicing gratitude has definite psychological and even physical benefits. When you show gratitude, it can increase your feelings of vitality and optimism, and reduce feelings of depression, while also giving your overall well-being a boost. Feeling grateful shifts your focus. We have been conversing about being focused since day one. If there is anything that can help you regain focus while trying to achieve your goals, that's a win.

If you aren't focused on being grateful, most likely your focus is geared toward negativity. I may have mentioned this every day: when you repeat yourself it creates belief, and belief creates manifestation, but being negative throws off your focus. STOP BEING NEGATIVE! You can go as far as you want to in life. Allowing yourself to be grateful and thankful for a lot of things that have gone on throughout your life and career will help you gain focus on the positive things in life.

If you have been journaling with me as you're reading this book, allow yourself some time daily to write down the reasons you are grateful.

You can write down what you are grateful for in life, your journey toward your success within your career, or in your entrepreneurship. Gratitude will boost your career or success rate.

As a manger I've learned to create a place where the morale results off showing gratitude. At the end of each day I make it my business to say thank you to each associate I encounter. If you show the employees who are in the trenches working day in and day out that you are truly honored to have them as part of your team it will make them want to come back and work harder each day. Marriott has a saying: "Take care of your associates, your associates will take care of your guests, and all of it will increase the bottom line." I wholeheartedly believe this. All people want to know that their hard work is noticed. I don't care if you have two dollars or a million dollars. If there isn't a sense of gratitude acknowledged for your hard work, you will ask yourself why you are doing what you do. Get those around you to buy into your vision. The buy-in creates success.

I am grateful for:

- Family
- Friends
- Health
- Where I have gotten in life
- The laughter that I still have inside me
- Discernment

The things I thought I wanted but God didn't give to me because it wasn't for me

What are you grateful for?

Day 23

"COMPLAINING GETS YOU NOWHERE. HARD WORK, DETERMINATION AND PERSISTENCE GETS YOU EVERYWHERE"

Once upon a time I had a Facebook page. On that page my tagline or quote I wrote that I try to live by was, "Complaining gets you nowhere. Hard work, determination, and persistence get you everywhere." Think about this statement. Let's break it down.

We have talked about so much in twenty-two days, of words or phrases that will help us become successful by breaking them down and internalizing them to create a journey tailored to our situation. Society seems to think that being successful can be cookie cutter. From my experience, everyone's success story is different. This book is designed to give you tools that can put your life into perspective, to motivate you, to get to YOUR success story.

Complaining is a hindrance. Complaining is negative energy. We discussed getting out what you put into the atmosphere. Complaining will not do anything for your journey because it will cloud your vision and bog down your mind when you could be using that space for positivity, focus, manifestation, and research anything other than focusing on things that are not beneficial to your journey.

Hard work. We discussed on day nine that nothing is given to any of us. Most of us build what we have through hard work. Through hard work there is progress. I've never seen a person work hard and not gain anything out of life. I've watched my parents work many jobs (especially my dad). They work sun up to sun down. I didn't see it as a child, but at thirty-one I am watching my parents have their dream home built from the ground up. Hard work got them there over time; it is the progress that you can visually see. There is no hard work that will go unnoticed. Never be afraid to outwork the competition. My mom went back to school at fifty, worked hard, graduated, and turned her life into what she envisioned for herself. Hard work! When you truly work hard, it gives you a sense of accomplishment. A part of you will always be proud to say, "I worked for this. It wasn't given."

Determination. After you stop complaining and start working hard, you develop a new mentality: the hunger and drive to get where you are trying to go creates the will. The will to succeed will make you unstoppable. Being determined has yet to fail anyone. It is funny to me that as I write about determination, the movie *Acrimony* by Tyler Perry comes to mind. If you haven't seen the movie, I won't spoil it for you, but I will tell you why determination comes to mind. The husband in the movie has an idea, a dream, and he goes through everything we've talked about thus far. He is told no, he endures letdowns, he works hard, he researches, he has passion, he reflects on things he's done wrong, but he never ever gives up, and after so long, that one yes he is waiting on is granted. Determination is what he has within him and persistence keeps him going. Persistence is key. Keep going. What if you give up right before your blessing is getting ready to occur? It is very hard at times, but if you do not take risk, you don't stand a chance at receiving the rewards.

Day 24

HOMAGE TO KOBE

"I have self-doubt. I have insecurities. I have a fear of failure. I have nights when I show up at the arena and I'm like, my back hurts, my feet hurt, my knees hurt. I don't have it. I just want to chill. We all have self-doubt. You don't deny it, but you also don't capitulate to it. You embrace it."

I am two days behind in writing this book, which was perfect to pay homage on day twenty-four to the number the great Kobe Bryant wore during his career of being one of the greatest to ever play the game of basketball. On January 26 we lost Kobe Bryant, his daughter, and nine others who were in a helicopter crash. I felt compelled by the heartache to research some of his quotes and tie them into our journey. I found the above quote from him and I couldn't help but to think to myself: "We all deal with the same exact insecurities. Even in our greatness there can arrive self-doubt." What Kobe taught us to do was tap into our gifts. No matter how we may be feeling at the time, we must embrace what we are given. At times even he, as great as he was, lacked focus, but because he was disciplined in his work, he worked hard through all of his obstacles. We never saw him make excuses. We saw someone determined to win, even if it meant putting the team on his back from time to time. He was about his work.

Kobe should be a lesson to all of us that when it comes to the will to win, to succeed in life, take things seriously and go after what you want. In some way we all just want to be great. We will have self-doubt. We will question our ability, but as Kobe said, embrace what you have. Turn your inability to ability. "Mamba out."

What gifts of yours have you not embraced?

Day 25

MENTAL CAPACITY

Mental capacity means you have the ability to make your own decisions. Within the process of becoming successful, it is very important to not listen to all the outside noise. Everyone will want to tell you how to go about making your dreams come true, but you can get lost in the mix of what everyone else thinks is best for you versus what you think is best for you. Taking care of your mental state is very important because you have to prepare yourself for transition. The transition from being a peer to achieving a level of elevation that you only dreamed of. Going through the process of becoming, there will be ups and downs, whirlwinds and rollercoaster swarms of emotions, but through it all, you have to take good care of yourself and your mental ability.

I've heard so many people say, "Success changes people." I have also heard the successor say money or success doesn't change them; it changes the people around them. How will you keep your mental health in check? I am a firm believer that you must try to prepare yourself for every outcome. Map out a plan; be upfront about your plan. Check your circle now, eliminate leeches, make sure the ones who are around now are hard workers and have a vision for themselves first. When you become that successful entrepreneur or business woman/man, etc., what will you do with your newfound success? Speak those things that are not as though they are. When you work hard for something and truly start to see the fruits of your labor, you do not have time to think about what the naysayers will have to say about you. Your priority should not be consumed with who will you take care of. Map out your plan now. Success starts with a plan, even if you hit a curve.

Mental check is OK. It is OK to see a therapist—again, an organized mind is a healthy mind that will allow you to create. There is a fine line between sane and insane. The mind also needs its rest and nourishment. I know early on I talked about sacrificing sleep, and it is perfectly fine to pull an all-nighter here and there, but do not get comfortable with that because rest is very important to your mental health and your creativity. Do not get caught in the hype listening to others say successful people do not sleep. A rested mind is a healthy creator.

Have you honestly been taking care of your mental being?

____

____

____

____

____

Have you thought about seeing a therapist? If so, what is stopping you from going?

____

____

____

____

____

____

What weight are you carrying around?

Day 26

NETWORKING

Networking is super important. New people can provide new opportunities. Staying social is good for your mental health. Your ability to pull resources will make you or break you. Networking is the key that can open plenty doors. It allows you to mingle with the who's who in the different markets. This can help you stay on top of the latest trends in your industry, or open a lane to a new venture.

We talked about how important it is to have a mentor. Maybe you don't have one but are in need of one. Networking puts you with experienced individuals who can guide you in the right direction.

Networking can help you in so many ways when it comes to being successful at anything. It is important to know a lawyer for legal advice. Insurance agents, all of the associates, are great to have when you're embarking upon success. An accountant is another important associate one may need when they become successful. There is an abundance of knowledge you can gain from having these types of business professionals around.

This may have been an idea of yours to get out there and network, so I will share some tips on how to do so:

- Use social media for networking events.
- Be nice to everyone you meet.
- Learn to communicate effectively.
- Ask questions.

- Observe.
- Figure out the types of professionals who will be beneficial to your goals.
- Be giving before you start to ask.
- Use Twitter, Facebook, and Instagram for the group pages.
- Build rapport.
- Be yourself, and most importantly, be confident.

What are you waiting for? Get up and find a few networking events to attend!

Day 27

INVEST

I know when people see the word invest they immediately only think in the terms of money, but truthfully, that is only one part of it. Investing in yourself and your ability comes in layers. Time is an investment that you can never get back. How you decide to spend your time is vital to your success. What you spend your time doing can help you in the long run. If you decided today that you will spend most of your time researching, networking, and working hard, don't you think that your investment will have a great return value to your bottom line? Invest: devote (one's time, effort, or energy) to a particular undertaking with the expectation of a worthwhile result.

Self-care is an investment we all should partake in. Our appearance is how we show the world exactly who we are or what we want to become before a word is spoken out of our mouths. If you are happy with how you present yourself to the world or at networking events, it will allow your confidence to shine through. When people see your confidence, they tend to gravitate toward you and want to work with you. Daily you should invest in how your hair looks, your face,—get a great skin-care routine together—and your choice of clothing. I cannot stress this enough: please pick the right clothing for the right environment. I interview people daily for jobs, and just being honest, if you show up to a job interview with club attire on, I tend to not take the person as seriously, mainly because the appearance has thrown my focus off. I am not telling you to go and spend a lot of money, but it does mean that a clean appearance will get you in the door. The thrift store is a great place to find cheaper clothing.

We touched on mental capacity, so make sure you invest in your health. It is very important to be healthy and happy on this journey. No, you will not be happy every single day, but you can choose to be emotionally stable daily. Invest in the future.

Now, let's talk about the money aspect. Being successful and breaking generational barriers is what most of us hope for. Land, bonds, stocks, and retirement plans are the biggest things you can invest in. I am not an expert, so you may want to do your own research before you make any drastic decisions. However, I do know that owning property is one of the better options. There's so much you can do with ownership.

What are you investing in?

___

___

___

___

___

___

___

___

___

___

___

Where will be your starting point, if you are not investing in anything at the moment?

Day 28

BRAINSTORMERS

Allow your creative juices to flow. A lot of times we think we should have everything figured out as soon as we have the idea that we want to prosper into our success. Unfortunately, it does not work that way, and we know this. We've been on this journey for twenty-eight days now. Brainstorming may allow you to come up with solutions to problems. Brainstorming can allow you to write out all your fears, doubts, and it will give you a visual representation of what you are trying to obtain. Brainstorming can build involvement, commitment, and enthusiasm. When you stay intrigued about your journey to success it allows you to want more, to stay hungry. It keeps you motivated to accomplish your goals.

There are a few things I want you to remember while brainstorming:

- Do not judge.
- Think with an open mind; nothing is off limits.
- Have others help in the process.
- The more input you have, the better.

Within the exercise of brainstorming, do not forget that it's a process of putting thoughts together to better your journey. I decided to talk about brainstorming so late in the journey because there is always time to refocus and look at everything you've done thus far. If you have been doing the work, you have been brainstorming. Each day was designed to make you think about your end goal. Every time I reread through this book, it allows me to brainstorm my way to my success. It allows me to look at my faults and imperfections, and perfect all aspects that I have control over.

Again, trust your process, but make it very clear that there will always be things to work through on your journey. Organize your thoughts, and continue to press forward. I have stated before: if I repeat something throughout the book, it is very important.

Day 29

REFLECTION DAY

After twenty-nine days of journaling, reflecting, and making changes to my life, I feel as though I'm on the right track to my own progression. I am not a millionaire, but I have hopes of manifesting all the things I want in life. Through this process I have gained a better perspective of my flaws and the challenges I've faced. I would love for you to do the same: reevaluate your life, reorganize, and take a different approach to your journey—it makes a world of difference. Are you truly trusting your process? I feel as though I am, but I am also human, and I tend to ask myself, "When is my time coming?" Through it all I remain focused on the task at hand. I'm currently trying to figure out the best route to take with Style Inc.

This book has been holding a lot of my attention, and I have brainstormed more ways to put Sh*ddd Let's Talk on the map.

All in all, I'm learning that I have come a long way from where I've been. I've always wanted to write a book and get it published. It is so much in me that I feel I can give to the world or other people like me a guide to helping achieve goals to being successful. At a certain point in your life you think of the what ifs, but I am at a point where I think: Why not me? Who said I couldn't be everything I'm destined to be? It is in me. I have all the ability in the world to be more, but it's up to me to take the tools I have presented here and place them in action. I have started bettering myself and keeping myself focused on my task, so I know soon my destiny will start to be fulfilled. I am promising myself to continue on my journey so that I can write my next book and tell you all that everything I envisioned for myself has manifested.

What have you learned after being truthful with yourself about your journey?

Day 30

RECIPROCITY

"Reciprocity refers to the social convention of returning in kind what we receive from others and expecting to respond similarly in regards to us." —422 business.com

In so many ways, success will come, but one way I have designed my life around knowing that one day my success will come through reciprocity. The good I do, or try my best to do, will always follow.

When we are young, we are taught the golden rule: treat others how you want to be treated. With social media, these days it's easy to show support to a starter company or a person starting out on a new journey with a career, to be the person who gives a simple shout-out or pours into someone else's dream. In theory, reciprocity tells us that one day the universe will return the favor.

In life we all look for the same thing, support being one of the biggest feelings we yearn for. Begin with putting great energy out into the world. At times I do things without thinking of myself; I genuinely love helping people. Therefore, I don't know when or how, but there will be a day where the energy I've put out into the world will align and all the reciprocity I've put into the world will return itself.

Day 31

PURPOSE

At the end of it all, we just want to know our purpose. What are we here on this earth to do? Purpose is the aim or goal of a person; what a person is trying to do or become. Hopefully through these exercises and reflection days you will come to conclusion of what drives you, what makes you happy, and figure out how to live out your purpose. I realized that I love fashion and writing more than I ever thought about. I learned that my desire to help others through words has been something I've yearned for and never realized.

As I talk to people about this book, I realize how happy I am to be putting together a guide that could potentially help a lot of people, some I may never meet and some I will, but my purpose—or at least one of my purposes—is to be able to really get through to people on their own level. I enjoy talking others into doing great things, so it feels amazing to put it into words through writing.

The only person can stop you from learning or getting to your purpose is you. Booker T. Washington once said, "Success is to be measured not so much by the position that one has reached in life as by the obstacles which he has overcome." Within finding our purpose we may endure obstacles, frustration, heartaches, and letdowns, as well as hear many nos, but we have learned to never give up, to press forward, work hard, and eventually, reciprocity will return in full force in the universe. Do the work, find your inner success, and take this with you.

"The purpose of life is not to be happy. It is to be useful, to be honorable, to be compassionate, and to have it make some difference that you have lived and lived well."
—Ralph Emerson

FINAL THOUGHT

I hope that the keys I have given you will unlock the doors of many ventures, as long as they lead you to success. Remember, nothing in this life is easy, but if you use the tools given to you, it will be a lot less difficult. I wish you well on your journey.

This journaling can be used over and over to help you navigate through life. Don't ever let someone tell you that you do not have purpose. You were designed for a specific reason on this earth; find it before you leave.

I truly believe that a purpose-driven life is a fulfilling life. K.E.Y.S. You have what you need. Just put the work and the action behind it. Faith without work is dead. Do the work!

ACKNOWLEDGMENTS

I would like take thank my parents, Daisy Clark and James and Mamie Coats, for making me the person I am today. They have always pushed me to do great things and taught me to never give up. My mother has always showed me strength and inspired me to express myself no matter what. My dad has taught me the value of hard work and discipline. My bonus mom, Mamie Coats, has shown me that you can go as far as the moon and the stars and even further if you do not place limits on your ability.

To my fiancé, Terry Lipscomb, thank you for believing in me when I didn't want to press forward. Thank you for teaching me things about me that I never knew. You contributed to us making a beautiful daughter; that I am more than grateful for. Together we will conquer the world. Kourtlynn, you have turned me into the woman I am supposed to become. Every day when I look into your eyes, you give me the motivation I need to be everything I pray for. I hope that I can be the best role model you will ever come across, through my actions and not just my words. On May 24, 2017, my life instantly changed, and I couldn't have prayed for better.

To Edna Coats and my deceased grandparents and my honorary moms, Mrs. Freda Wilson, Diane Harrell, and Debbie Moore, thank you all for contributing to my overall success. Thank you for showing me what it's like to be a stand-up person and to stay true to who I am.

To my sisters and brothers, Lady, Shaunda, Ant, Moody, Sweetah, Lamark Stinson (may you rest in peace), Trea, and nieces and nephews Ashia, David, Avah, Jaheim, Diamond, MarMar, and Jaiden, you all give me so much grief because you all know exactly how much potential I carry. Man, it's hard to explain our bond because it's so different from other siblings'. I know you all gone ride—right, wrong, or indifferent. Each of you speaks life into me. I think that's why I know I have to make a way for all of us to make it out. When I make it, we all make it. PERIOD!

To the Clark/Coats family: aunts Rosie, Dorothy, Julean, Veronica; uncles Red Corey Joe, R.I.P. Uncle Boobie, Clarence, Chris, Tony, and Fredrick, Uncle Rufus, Uncle Sonny; and cousins. Thank you for the times you stepped in when I needed support. This is an opportunity to enlighten generations to come, and I couldn't have done it without your help.

To my friends, in no particular order: Miyla, Lee-Lee, Radhia, Chiquita, Danielle, Chelle, Angela (BunBun), Robby, Markisha, Cimmie, Rashaunda, Jessica, Marvalyn, Tim, and bro Terry, you have all inspired me to keep my head held high and do what comes naturally. Each of you inspire me in different ways, but please know you contribute to my success in more ways than you think.

To everyone I acknowledged, thank you sooooo much and I love you all.

To my God, my provider: I cannot thank you enough. You created a great being when you created me. There are not enough words to describe my feelings toward my most high, but I owe you all the gratitude in the world.

www.ingramcontent.com/pod-product-compliance
Ingram Content Group UK Ltd.
Pitfield, Milton Keynes, MK11 3LW, UK
UKHW020422250726
13967UKWH00007B/2772

9 781641 119122